ORLAND PARK PUBLIC LIBRARY
14921 Ravinia Avenue
Orland Park, Illinois 60462
708-428-5100

Tending the Tide Pool:
The Parts Make a Whole

by Donna Loughran

Content Consultant
David T. Hughes
Mathematics Curriculum Specialist

NORWOOD HOUSE PRESS
Chicago, IL

Norwood House Press
PO Box 316598
Chicago, IL 60631

For information regarding Norwood House Press, please visit our website at
www.norwoodhousepress.com or call 866-565-2900.

Special thanks to: Heidi Doyle
Production Management: Six Red Marbles
Editors: Linda Bullock and Kendra Muntz
Printed in Heshan City, Guangdong, China. 208N—012013

Library of Congress Cataloging–in-Publication Data

Loughran, Donna.

    Tending the tide pool: the parts make a whole / by Donna Loughran;
consultant, David T. Hughes, math curriculum specialist.
pages cm.—(iMath)

    Summary: "The mathematical concepts of finding and naming equal parts are
introduced as children volunteer for a day at the local aquarium. Readers
learn about partitions, arrays, and number sentences, as well as parts of a
whole and skip counting. This book also features a discover activity, a
connection to art, and a mathematical vocabulary introduction"—Provided
by publisher.

Includes bibliographical references and index.

ISBN: 978-1-59953-555-5 (library edition: alk. paper)
ISBN: 978-1-60357-524-9 (ebook) (print)

1. Whole and parts (Psychology)—Juvenile literature.
2. Arithmetic—Juvenile literature. I. Title.

BF202.L68 2012
513.2'4—dc23
2012035747

CONTENTS

Note to Caregivers:

Throughout this book, many questions are posed to the reader. Some are open-ended and ask what the reader thinks. Discuss these questions with your child and guide him or her in thinking through the possible answers and outcomes. There are also questions posed which have a specific answer. Encourage your child to read through the text to determine the correct answer. Most importantly, encourage answers grounded in reality while also allowing imaginations to soar. Information to help support you as you share the book with your child is provided in the back in the **Additional Notes** section.

Bold words are defined in the glossary in the back of the book.

Share and Share Alike

Let's take a trip to the **aquarium**! An aquarium is a place with large glass tanks. The tanks are filled with animal life.

The Seaside Aquarium is my favorite place to go. It is built on a beach. The beach is part of the aquarium. I like to watch the birds that run on the sand. My favorite outdoor animals are the big seals that sleep on rocks.

There are lots of things to see inside the aquarium, too. Look at the fish tank in the photograph. Its large window has three parts. Each part is the same size. All of the parts make a **whole** window.

In this book, you will see how parts of things make up a whole. You will also learn a lot about animals at the aquarium!

iMath **Ideas**

The Parts Make a Whole

A **share** is a part of a whole. Parts that have the same amount are **equal**. There are different ways to find and name how much we have.

Idea 1: Find and Name Equal Parts. Look at the equal parts in each circle. You can name them.

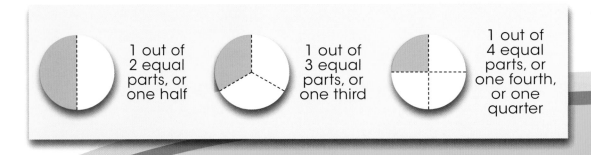

1 out of 2 equal parts, or one half

1 out of 3 equal parts, or one third

1 out of 4 equal parts, or one fourth, or one quarter

Look at the box of shells. It has three equal parts. Name how many parts are empty.

Is finding and naming equal parts a good way to show how much we have? Why or why not?

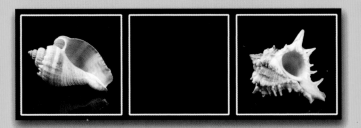

Idea 2: Make an Array. You can make an **array** to find how many parts there are in all. An array is a set of objects. The objects are put in rows. The same number of objects is in each row. Look at this array. You can write two **number sentences** to show how many fish are in the array.

4 + 4 = 8
2 + 2 + 2 + 2 = 8

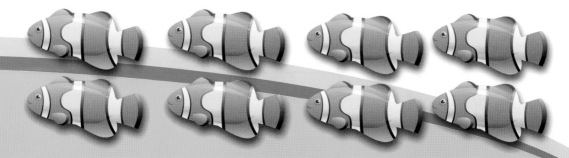

You can also **skip count** to show how many fish are in the array. You skip count when you count on by a number greater than one.

Skip count on by 4: 4, 8
Skip count on by 2: 2, 4, 6, 8

Is an array a good way to show how many we have in all? Why or why not?

7

Discover Activity

Go Fish

Work with a family member. Draw five fish on colored paper. Make each fish a different color. Cut some of the fish into three parts. Cut others into four parts. Then, tape a pipe cleaner loop onto the top of each part. Look at the pictures for examples.

Materials
- colored paper
- colored markers
- safety scissors
- paper clips
- tape
- pipe cleaners
- string
- bowl

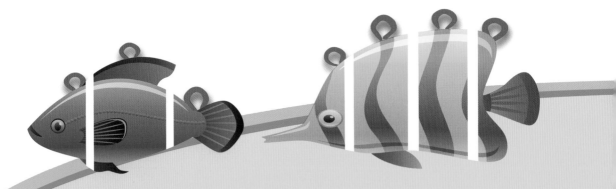

Now, make your fishing pole. Tie a paper-clip hook to a string. Put the fish parts in a bowl. Now, go fish! Take turns fishing for all of the pieces of one fish. Complete as many fish as you can, with all of the parts making a whole.

Volunteer Day

My parents bring me to the aquarium for "**Volunteer** Day." A volunteer is someone who offers to help. My friend Mary and her brother Diego are volunteers, too.

"Welcome! I'm Paloma," a worker says. "Thank you for helping me today. There is a lot to do! One of our jobs will be to build a special pool. Take some time to look around first.
Then, we will start our work."

This large, grumpy-looking fish is called a grouper.

Diego sees a fish in the tank. It looks grumpy, like his sister. Mary really wants to be here today. But, she doesn't like to wake up early.

"Look, Mary," says Diego. "That fish looks grumpy, just like you!"

"*Tanks* very much," says Mary, laughing.

Building a Tide Pool

"Let me explain about the special pool we are going to build," Paloma says. "The ocean moves in. Then, it moves out. It does this two times each day. These movements are called **tides**."

"When tides come in, water covers the beach. When they go out, sea animals are left behind in puddles of water. These puddles are called **tide pools**."

This tide pool is filled with red sea stars, shelled animals, and green sea flowers.

"We are going to use a box to make a tide pool. The box has four equal parts. We will carry water from the ocean to fill them," says Paloma.

I fill one part of the box. What part of the box did I fill?

We fill the rest of the parts with water. "Now let's put some animals in the tide pool," says Paloma.

"What about **sea stars**?" I ask. "They are interesting animals."

"Good thinking," says Paloma. "Sea stars are safe and easy for people to hold. Come with me. We'll get some from the tide pools outside."

We each come back with a sea star. Paloma, Mary, and Diego each put theirs into a different part of the pool. What part of the sea stars are in the pool?

Think what you could do with five arms! Most sea stars, like this one, have five arms. But, some can have ten or twenty!

"I saw some **crabs** outside, Paloma," says Mary. "Do they live in tide pools?"

"Yes, some do," Paloma says. She points to an animal in a tank. "This is a hermit crab," she explains. "It lives in shells that other animals leave behind."

This array shows how many legs a crab has. How many legs does it have in all? Add or skip count to find the number of legs.

A hermit crab can grow too big for its shell. So, it finds a new one.

"Let's stop our work for now. It's time to feed the **penguins**," says Paloma. "You will like these funny birds. Later, we will add more animals to our tide pool."

Paloma's Penguins

Aquarium visitors wait at the penguin pen. They want to watch Paloma feed the penguins. Three penguins are waiting, too. They begin to flap their wings and honk.

Paloma gives each of us a bucket of fish. "Each penguin gets one bucket of fish," she says. "Hold the fish between your thumb and a finger. Let it slide into the penguin's mouth."

Penguins are birds. But they do not fly.

"What fun!" I laugh. Mary and Diego's penguins eat all of their fish. Their buckets are soon empty. But my penguin wants to play first. My bucket is still full.

What part of the buckets are still full?

What's the Word?

Do you know what a tongue twister is? It is a sentence that is hard to say aloud. It is a way to have fun with words.

Read this tongue twister. Then, try to say it more than once. Say it as fast as you can.

Sally sells seashells at the seashore.

Now try another.

Paloma petted perky penguins.

Can you make up your own tongue twister about an aquarium?

You *Otter* Eat

"Let's feed the **sea otters** now," Paloma says.

Diego says, "We *otter* look after the otters." Everyone laughs.

"What do sea otters eat?" I ask.

"They eat fish and crabs. But they like **abalone** [ab-uh-LOH-nee] a lot."

This otter eats while floating.

"I like baloney, too," Diego says.

"Not baloney, Diego," answers Paloma. "Abalone. It's a sea animal. It lives inside a shell."

We each carry two buckets of fish. How many buckets do we have in all?

Math at Work

Divers work at aquariums. Divers use math to stay safe under the water.

A diver wears a tank. It is filled with air. She puts a hose in her mouth. She breathes in air from her tank.

Each breath takes air out of the diver's tank. So, she must read numbers to know how much air is left to breathe.

A diver helps keep a tank clean.

Divers also read numbers to keep track of how deep in the water they are. It is not safe to go too deep.

A diver reads a watch to know how long she is under the water. She must leave enough time to get back to the top safely.

Chihuly uses many colors and shapes in his art.
What does this art make you think of?

Connecting to Art

Dale Chihuly is an artist. He works with glass. He loves the ocean. He thinks glass looks like water. He uses glass to make sea animal art. He shows his art in museums.

In a museum, Chihuly puts some glass shapes on the floor. He puts others above a glass ceiling. Visitors in the museum walk beneath the ceiling. They look up at the glass shapes. It is like looking up from the bottom of the ocean.

Stinging Sea Flowers

"We have fed the penguins. And we have fed the otters. Now it is time to put more animals in our tide pool," says Paloma. "We can add some **sea flowers**."

She shows us the animals with the waving arms. "We call those arms tentacles (TEN-tuh-kuhlz). They have stingers in them.

The real name for a sea flower is sea anemone (uh-NEM-uh-nee).

A sea flower waits for a fish to swim by. Then, it stings the fish and pulls it into its mouth."

"Cool!" we all say at the same time.

How many sea flowers does Paloma put in the tide pool? Add or skip count to find out.

ⓘMath **Ideas: Parts and a Whole**

The day ends too soon. On our way out, we see a **stingray**.

"That animal makes me think of someone who jokes a lot!" Mary says.

Paloma walks us to the shop so we can look for gifts. She points to a box of seashells. The box has two equal parts. "Some of the shells are missing from the box. What part of the box is filled with shells?"

A stingray spends most of its time on the seafloor. It lays flat and covered with sand.

To find out, we can:

Find and Name Equal Parts. The box has two equal parts. How much of the box is empty?

We see another box, and it looks full. "How many shells are there in this box?" Paloma asks next.

Make an Array. The children take the shells from the box. They make an array to count. First, they write a number sentence to add up the shells. Then, they skip count to check their answer. How many shells are there in all?

"What a great day!" I tell my parents. Mary tells them about the tide pool. Diego tells them about the smelly fish. "The penguins ate every one of them!" he says.

We all laugh. I hope we come back to the aquarium soon. I would like to volunteer again!

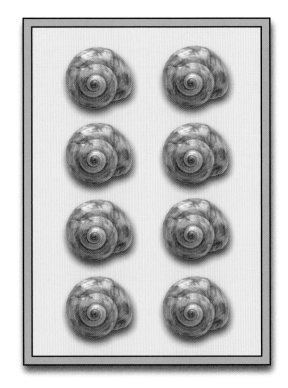

What Comes Next?

Do you collect shells? Or do you collect rocks or colorful seeds? What about tiny toys? Collecting can be fun. It's like being on a treasure hunt that lasts forever.

An array is a good way to show your treasures. You can build an array out of many things. Get an empty egg tray, for example. Or use an empty egg carton. Paint and decorate your array.

Then, put one object in each cup of the tray. What you see is an array.

Use the array to count the treasures in your collection.

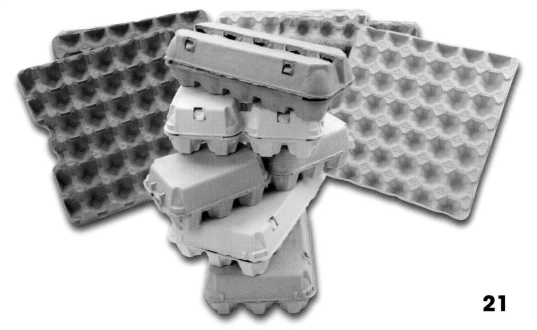

GLOSSARY

abalone: a shellfish that otters eat.

aquarium: tank that holds water and fish; a place that has and teaches about sea animals.

array: a set of objects in equal rows and equal columns.

crab: a shore animal with ten legs. The front two legs have claws.

equal: having the same amount.

number sentence: a sentence that uses numbers. 3 + 2 = 5 is a number sentence.

penguin: a sea bird that does not fly.

sea flower: also called an anemone; an underwater animal with a round, sticky foot, finger-like body parts, and a mouth.

sea otter: a sea animal that has waterproof fur, tiny ears, and a long tail.

sea stars: also called starfish; sea animals that have many arms. Most have five arms, but some have ten or twenty.

shares: parts of a whole.

skip count: to count forward or backward by a number greater than 1.

stingray: a flat fish with a long tail. A stingray is part of the shark family.

tide: a flow of water that moves in from the ocean and back out again twice a day.

tide pool: a rock pool near the sea that has sea animals living in it.

volunteer: a person who helps others by working for free.

whole: all of one thing.

FURTHER READING

FICTION

Full House: An Invitation to Fractions, by Dayle Ann Dodds, Candlewick, 2009

Ocean's Child, by Christine Ford and Trish Holland, Golden Books, 2009

NONFICTION

A Fraction's Goal: Parts of a Whole, by Brian P. Cleary, Millbrook Press, 2011

Baby Sea Otter, by Betty Tatham, Henry Holt, 2005

Additional Notes

The page references below provide answers to questions asked throughout the book. Questions whose answers will vary are not addressed.

Page 6: 1 out of 3 parts, or one third

Page 10: 1 out of 4 parts, or one fourth, or one quarter

Page 11: 3 out of 4 parts, or three fourths, or three quarters

Page 12: 10 legs

Page 13: 1 out of 3 buckets, or one third

Page 15: 8 buckets of fish

Page 18: 9 sea flowers

Page 19: 1 out of 2 parts, or one half

Page 20: Add: $2 + 2 + 2 + 2 = 8$. Skip count: 2, 4, 6, 8. There are 8 shells.

INDEX

Content Consultant

David T. Hughes

David is an experienced mathematics teacher, writer, presenter, and adviser. He serves as a consultant for the Partnership for Assessment of Readiness for College and Careers. David has also worked as the Senior Program Coordinator for the Charles A. Dana Center at The University of Texas at Austin and was an editor and contributor for the *Mathematics Standards in the Classroom* series.